THIS BOOK THINKS YOU'RE A SCIENTIST

EXPERIMENT IMAGINE CREATE

FILL-IN PAGES FOR YOUR IDEAS

ILLUSTRATED BY HARRIET RUSSELL

Thames & Hudson

Answer to the puzzle of Farmer John,
the fox, the chicken and the corn from
page 26:

First Farmer John takes the chicken across the river,
leaving the fox and corn together. He leaves the chicken
on the bank, and rows back to the fox and the corn.

He collects the fox, and takes it across the river.
He can't leave the chicken and fox together,
so he leaves the fox and picks up the chicken.

He rows back over to the corn, leaves the chicken
on the bank, and takes the corn over the river.
He drops the corn off with the fox, and returns back
over the river for one last trip to collect the chicken.

The activities in this book were inspired by Wonderlab: The Statoil Gallery at the Science Museum, London.
See them brought to life with a visit to this major interactive gallery.
Find out more at: www.sciencemuseum.org.uk/wonderlab
Every purchase supports the museum.

With special thanks to Toby Parkin, Natalie Mills, Thomas Woolley and Harry Cliff.

Produced in association with Science Museum SCIENCE MUSEUM ® SCMG

This Book Thinks You're a Scientist © 2016 Thames & Hudson Ltd, London

First published in 2016 in the United States of America by
Thames & Hudson Inc., 500 Fifth Avenue, New York, New York 10110

thamesandhudsonusa.com

Library of Congress Catalog Card Number 2016931257

ISBN 978-0-500-65081-3

Printed and bound in China by Everbest Printing Co. Ltd

THIS BOOK THINKS YOU'RE A SCIENTIST

ILLUSTRATED BY HARRIET RUSSELL

Yes, you!

You don't need test tubes or Bunsen burners or fancy machines to be a scientist. Your mission is simply to LOOK closely at the world, pay ATTENTION and ASK QUESTIONS.

Once you start looking, you'll notice PATTERNS and details that you didn't spot before. You'll start to WONDER why things are the way they are, and come up with possible answers. You can find ways to TEST your ideas and then – hey! You're a scientist!

CONTENTS

Learn to Look

Forces and Motion

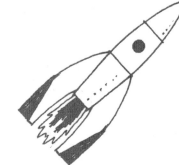

Mathematics

$$E = mc^2$$

Earth and Space

DRAW YOURSELF AND YOUR SIDEKICK

You are the Super Scientists, Caped Crusaders of Curiosity!

DO THIS!

Design your outfits and invent some Super Science gadgets.

List your Super Skills:
-Pinpoint accuracy
-Tireless curiosity

Invent and draw your
Super Science gadget here.
How about a Measure-Anything Ray Gun?

BECOME THE WORLD EXPERT ON A RANDOM OBJECT

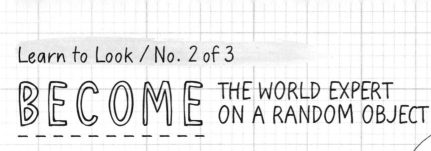

DO THIS!

1st Choose any random object from your house.

I'm feeling pretty random!

2nd Draw it here in as much detail as you possibly can:

Label every bit of your object with a word that describes it.

Bowl

Shiny

Handle

Metal

Don't stare so hard your eyes fall out...

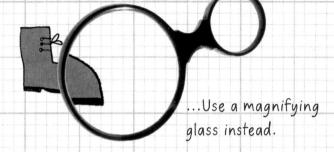

...Use a magnifying glass instead.

DO THIS!

Fill in this Scientific Fact Sheet:

Most POINTLESS fact I know about this object:

FUNNIEST joke I can make up using this object:

What my object smells like when I SNIFF it:

THREE THINGS I don't know about this object:
1

SILLIEST way this object could be used:

2

3

What my object will be doing in 10 YEARS time:

WRITE YOUR RANDOM OBJECT REPORT

MEGA WARNING:
Breaking objects that don't belong to you will only test your parents' patience!

DO THIS!

Conduct scientific tests on your random object.
Come up with ways to measure and test it, and record your results here:

How heavy is your object?

....

How hot is it?

....

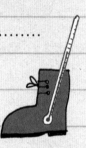

How high does it bounce when you drop it?

....

Does it reflect light?
YES/NO

Does it change if you freeze it?
YES/NO

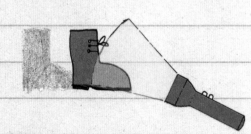

DO THIS!

Sometimes it's not possible to measure something exactly. When you make a close guess of the size or amount of something by figuring it out instead of measuring it, it's called "estimating."

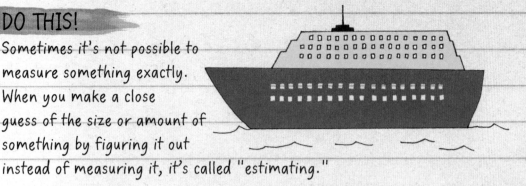

Draw wacky ways to estimate the size of really big things, like:

How many elephants you could fit in your house...

Or how many umbrellas it would take to keep the Statue of Liberty dry...

RUN TESTS ON YOURSELF BY RUNNING

DO THIS!

Run around your house or the park, and draw on this page all the moving things you can see.

Only rule: you must draw WHILE running!

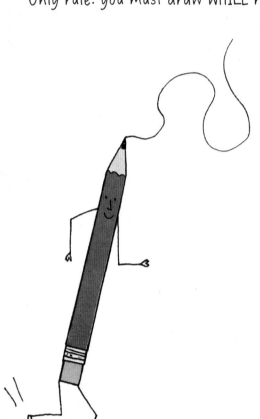

MEGA WARNING:
Keep looking around you as you run!
Take care not to run into any people,
lamp posts, cats, or banana peels...

How does the movement affect your drawing? Try drawing
straight lines here while walking, running and jumping:

Line drawn while walking:

Line drawn while running:

Line drawn while jumping:

HOW IT WORKS

Forces are always found in pairs, so
every "action" has an equal and opposite
"reaction." When you walk or run, your
foot pushes downwards on the ground,
but at the same time, the ground pushes
upwards on your foot. The stronger
the downwards force, the stronger
the upwards push-back.

Reaction

Action

INVESTIGATE HOW FAR YOU CAN TIP FORWARD

HUGE WARNING:
Be extra careful

DO THIS!

1st   Make a big, soft landing place.
      Be careful as you tip forward!

2nd   Test how far you can lean.
      What's your tipping point?

HOW WILL YOU MEASURE YOUR LEAN?

It's tricky! You could ...
... shout "Geronimooo!" slowly.
... or design your own lean-ometer.

Leaning Tower of Pisa

THE LEAN-OMETER

Think beyond your feet! Balance on different parts of your body.

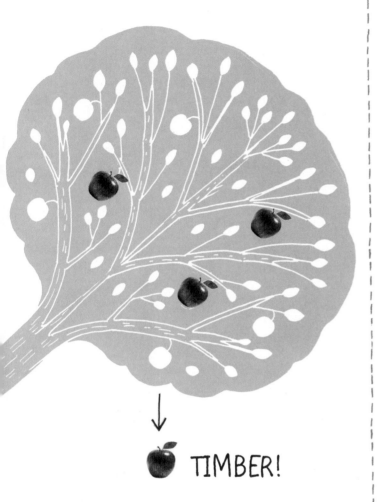

↓

🍎 TIMBER!

DO THIS!

Try tipping-point poses.
Are they easy or difficult?

the superhero

☐   1 = easy
10 = difficult

the gymnast ☐   the invisible chair ☐

the upside-downer ☐   the bird ☐

HOW IT WORKS

Every object, including our bodies, has a center of gravity. This is the exact point that our weight is evenly spread around. As you start to lean over, your center of gravity is no longer over your feet. Your weight is not supported and you fall over.

Sir Isaac Newton discovered gravity.

SLIDE A COIN DOWN THIS PAGE

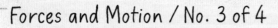

DO THIS!

1st

Collect some pieces of different materials from around your house, such as tin foil, plastic wrap, or fabric. Glue strips onto these slides.

2nd

Hold the book at an angle and slide a coin down each one on its side. Which slide is the fastest?

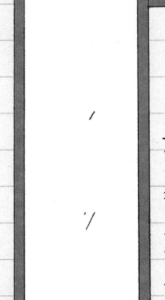

HOW IT WORKS

Friction is a force that slows down sliding objects. Some surfaces create more friction than others. The smoother a surface is, the less friction it creates.

Stick strips of material along these slides

Material

. . . .

Material

. . . .

What else can you change to make your coin slide faster or slower?

Material

. . . .

MOVE THIS BOOK AS FAR AS YOU CAN

DO THIS!

Invent a way to move this book as far as you can in one go. Think about the forces you already know about and try to use them to help move your book.

Blow

You could try using other objects to help move your book. Can you make your book roll using pencils as wheels?

Can you use a ruler to lever your book?

Fly

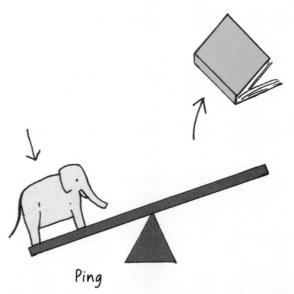

Ping

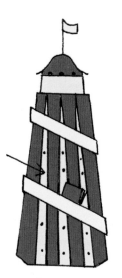

Slide

Draw your own book-moving method here:

Roll

HOW IT WORKS
An object that is moving has "momentum." This means the object will keep going unless another force stops it, like friction or air resistance.

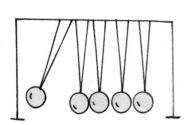

DRAW AN INFINITE FRACTAL PATTERN

DO THIS!

Add branches to the fern at even points along each existing branch. Then add new smaller branches to those branches, and so on.

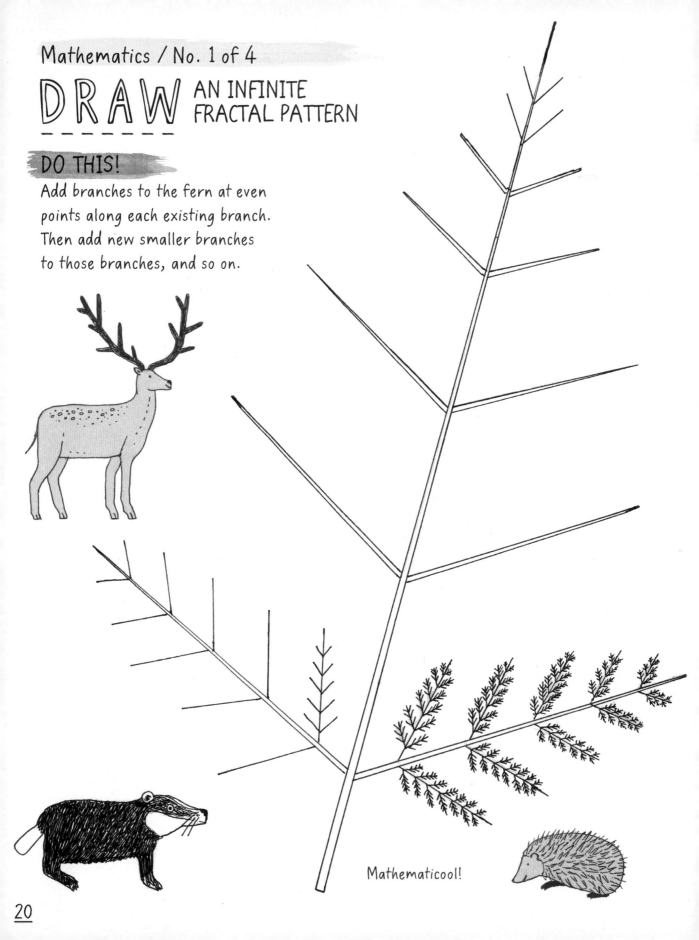

Mathematicool!

HOW IT WORKS

A fractal is a pattern with "self-similarity."
This means a small part of the shape looks
like the whole shape when you zoom in.

Self-similar shapes appear a lot in
nature, for example in ferns, or shells
when you zoom into the center.

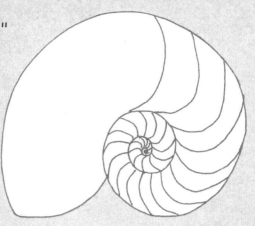

DO THIS!

Complete this Sierpinski Triangle
fractal. Draw upside-down
triangles inside every upright
triangle, until you can't draw
any smaller.

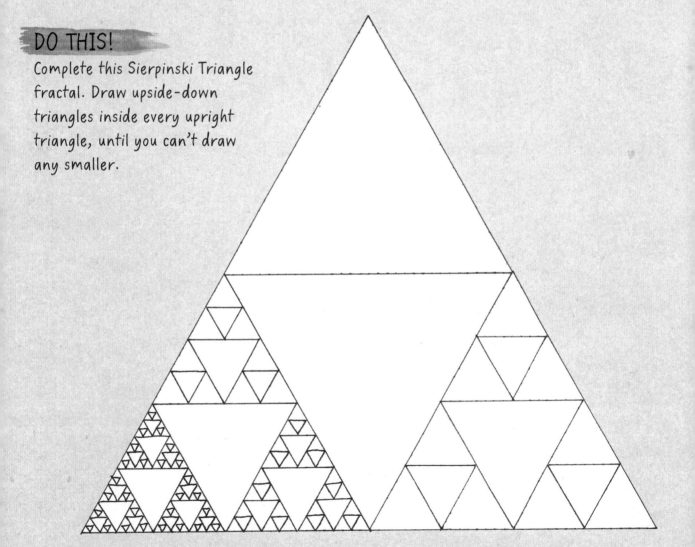

THINK ABOUT

HOW TO FIT THE MOST PEOPLE ON THIS BUS

People can stand, sit or lie down.
Squeeze in as many as possible.

Hey – you're
squashing me!

Bend and curl your
people into odd positions.

Ouch!
My foot!

DO THIS!

1st   Practice drawing your people here.

2nd   Now cram lots inside the bus shape.

HOW IT WORKS

When you arrange shapes next to each other with with no empty space, it's called tessellation.

DO THIS!

Go to page 73.
Cut out the shapes.
Draw around them here:

TESSELLATION TEST BED

😊 cosy

😐 in-between

☹ uncomfortable

DO THIS!

Which shapes tessellate? Which don't? Rate them!

○ ○ ○ ○ ○ ○

COLOR THIS MATH PUZZLE

Here's an example - only three colors needed!

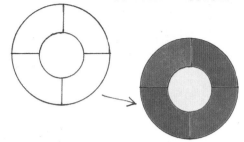

DO THIS!

Color in these shapes using the smallest possible number of colors, so that no two spaces share an edge of the same color. (Touching at a corner is OK.)

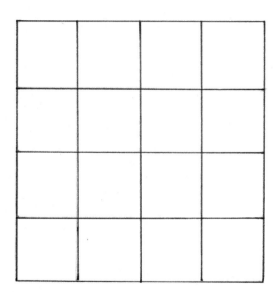

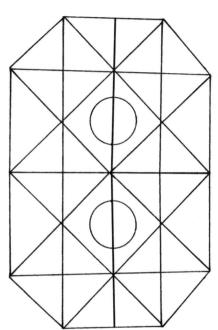

What is the minimum number of colors you need?

What is the maximum?

Try coloring this squiggle:

HOW IT WORKS

For any shape, the maximum number of colors you will need is four. Yes, really! The mathematical explanation for this is called the Four Color Theorum.

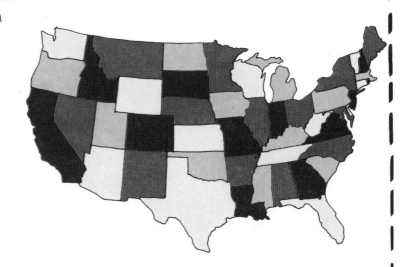

SOLVE THE PUZZLE OF FARMER JOHN, THE FOX, THE CHICKEN AND THE CORN

DO THIS!

Help Farmer John! He needs to get his fox, his chicken and his corn across a river. He has a row-boat, but it can only carry him and one other thing.

If the chicken is left alone with the fox, the fox will eat it. If the chicken is left with the corn, the chicken will eat the corn...

How can he do it?

Hmm.... tricky...

Take the corn first. I won't eat the chicken... promise!

Answer on page 2

Cluck, cluck

If it helps, draw little pictures of the farmer, fox, chicken and corn on some paper and cut them out. Move them around the page as you think the puzzle through.

HOW IT WORKS

This might not look like the sort of mathsyou do at school, because it doesn't contain sums or numbers. But this sort of reasoning is an important part of math used in real-world situations, like computer programming.

1001101110 0
011 0110101 011
00111010101 011
1100110011001

DESIGN SOME NEW CONSTELLATIONS FOR THE NIGHT SKY

DO THIS!

Look at this star map, and draw lines between the stars to create your own constellations. Look out for your patterns in the night sky.

I name that one "Bob."

HOW IT WORKS

Since the earliest times, people have seen patterns in the stars, and given them names. Because stars change position throughout the year, people used to use the stars to tell them when to plant and harvest crops.

IMAGINE YOU CAN MOVE THE EARTH

DO THIS!

Draw a comic strip in which you are an evil genius who can move the Earth closer to or further away from the sun.

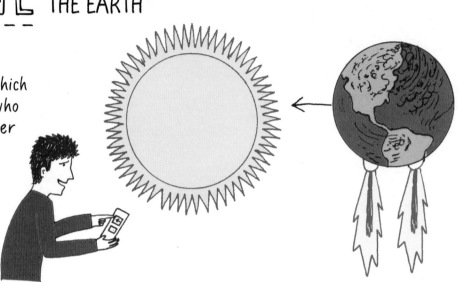

What's the comic's title?

What's the first thing you do?

What happens at the North and South pole?

What happens to your home town?

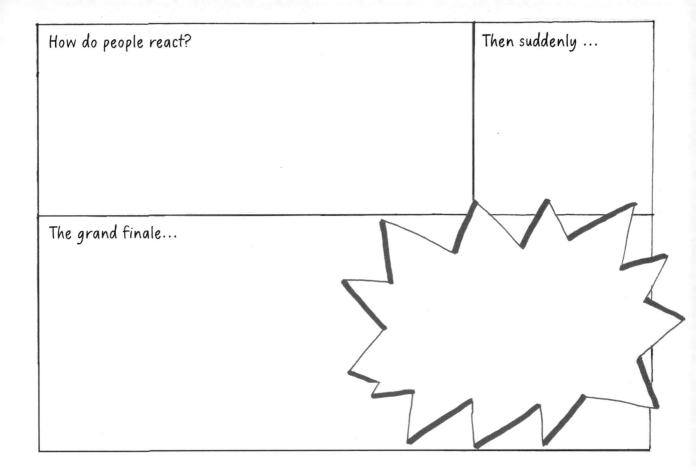

How do people react?

Then suddenly ...

The grand finale...

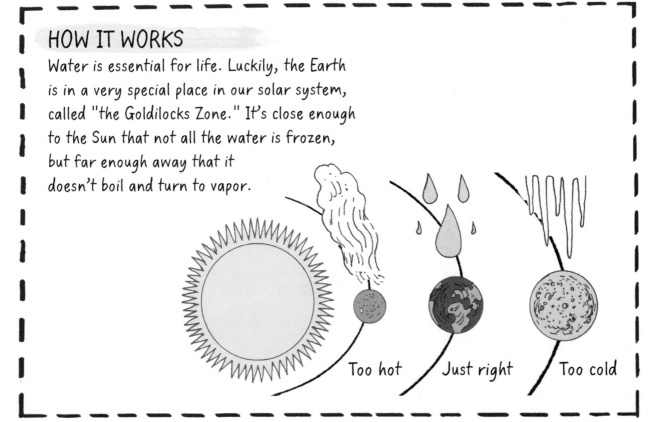

HOW IT WORKS

Water is essential for life. Luckily, the Earth
is in a very special place in our solar system,
called "the Goldilocks Zone." It's close enough
to the Sun that not all the water is frozen,
but far enough away that it
doesn't boil and turn to vapor.

Too hot   Just right   Too cold

DRAW THE MOON IN AS MUCH DETAIL AS YOU CAN

DO THIS!

Go outside and look at the Moon.
Use a telescope or binoculars if
you have them. Study the patterns
on the surface, and draw
them here:

I can see the Moon's backside!

The word "month" comes from "moon-th."

Do I look like a man to you?

Some cultures don't see a "Man in the Moon," they see a rabbit instead.

Draw what the Moon looks like every day for one month.

This moon chart was recorded in the month of ....

HOW IT WORKS

The way the Moon moves around the Earth makes it look like it is changing shape in the sky.

Turn to page 76 to make a model showing how the Moon, Earth and Sun move.

PACK A SUITCASE FOR A TRIP TO SPACE

DO THIS!

Imagine you are an astronaut about to spend one month in space. Draw all the items you will need to take with you to live life without Earth's gravity.

Oh no, I forgot my toothbrush!

HOW IT WORKS

Simple things like eating, sleeping, and going to the toilet are much more complicated in weightless space stations. Astronauts have to be strapped down to sleep, and food seasonings like salt and pepper are put into liquid to stop the individual grains floating away.

CHECK THIS COLOR CHART AGAINST THINGS YOU FIND

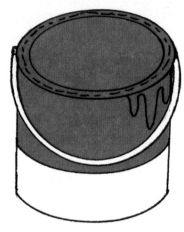

DO THIS!

1st Find scraps of stuff that exactly match the colors on these cans. Stick the scraps on the matching color.

2nd Label the colors in the style of paint names, like "Volcano Breeze" or "Mermaid's Toenail." The sillier the better.

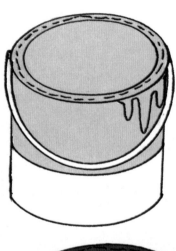

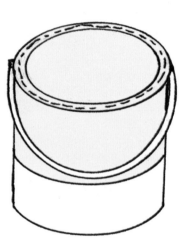

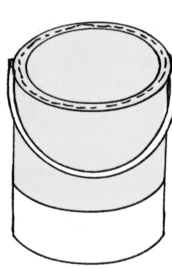

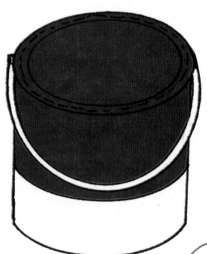

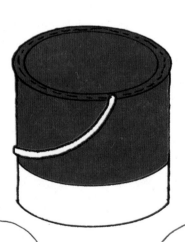

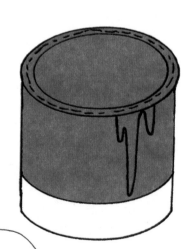

That color is so you!

Help, I'm stuck!

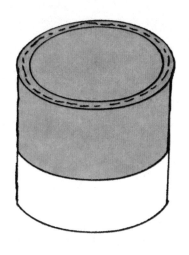

DO THIS!

When you have completed your color chart, look at it through a colored lens. A colored plastic bottle would work for this. How do the colors look different?

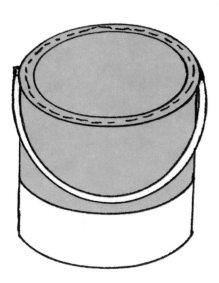

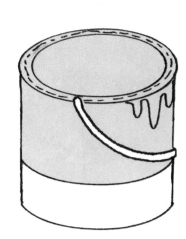

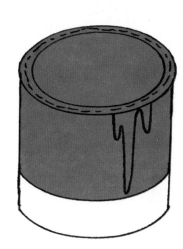

HOW IT WORKS

Things around us appear different colors because they reflect light into our eyes in different ways. Normal white light is actually a mixture of all the colors. Looking through a colored lens filters out parts of the white light, so colors appear changed.

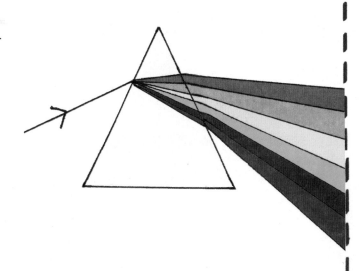

TAKE INSTANT PHOTOGRAPHS WITH YOUR EYES

MEGA WARNING:
Never look directly at the Sun!
The Sun is easily offended, and
also it will damage your eyes.

DO THIS!

Stare at a distant light source
like a window (NOT the Sun!) for
10 seconds. Shut your eyes and
look at the after-image on your
eyelids. Now try and draw the
after-image in the boxes below.

Wow! What happens if you try blinking?

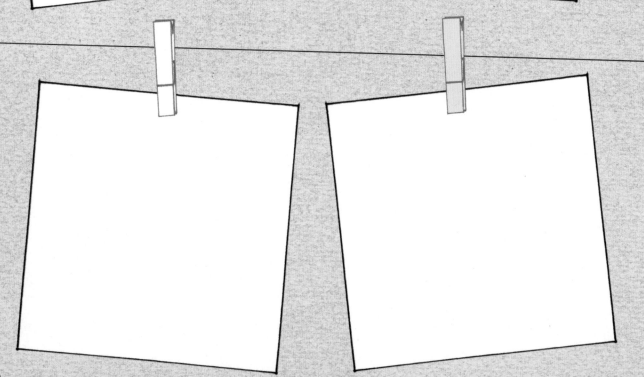

DO THIS!

In a well-lit room, stare at the dot in the center of this flag for 20 seconds. Then lightly shut your eyes. What can you see?

DO THIS!

Draw your own solid shape in black marker pen in this box. Stare at it in bright light for 20 seconds, then gently shut your eyes.

HOW IT WORKS

There are color-sensitive cells in your eyes. If you stare at one color for a long time, those cells need to recharge. And when you look away, they don't work very well, so you see the opposite of what you were looking at.

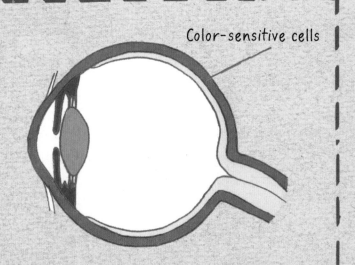

Color-sensitive cells

LOOK

AT YOURSELF

mirror

BETWEEN TWO MIRRORS

mirror

How small is the smallest you?

DO THIS! Draw how you look between two mirrors.

How many "yous" do you see?

Hello there!

Speak up!

It's not easy drawing mirror selves inside each other. Don't worry if it looks weird, it IS weird!

Look who's behind you.

DO THIS!
Strike mirror poses.

pull
faces

A-ttention!

wibble

wobble

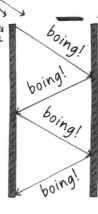

light

boing!

boing!

boing!

boing!

HOW IT ALL WORKS
Light bounces off the first mirror
then off the second. Each mirror
reflects everything seen in the other,
including itself. It looks like each
mirror goes on forever.

CREATE AN OBSTACLE COURSE FOR LIGHT

DO THIS!

Find things that reflect, distort, let through or filter light. Build an obstacle course and try to bounce a beam of light through it.

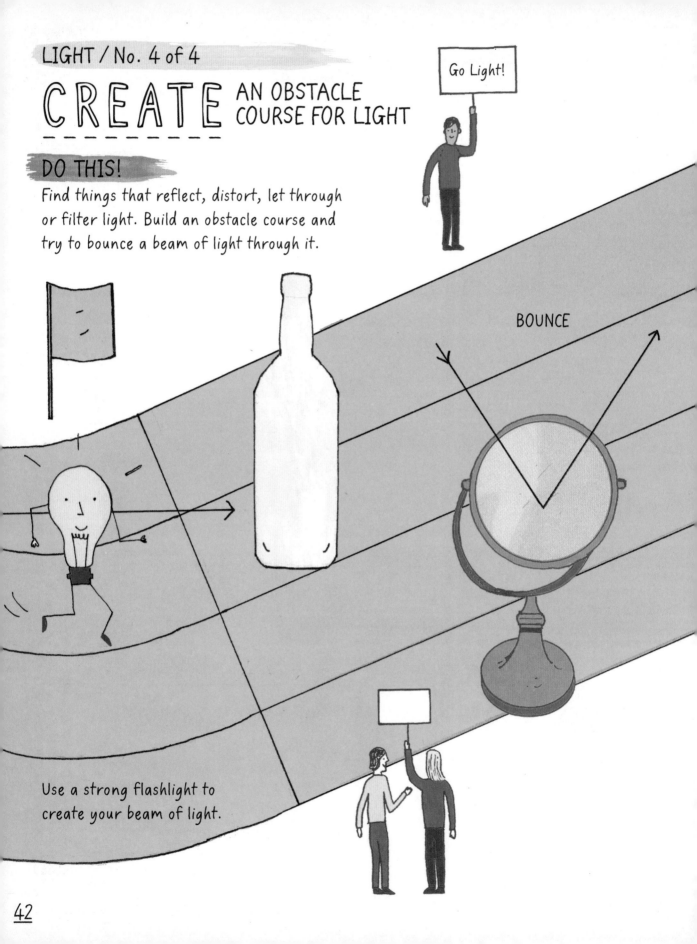

Go Light!

BOUNCE

Use a strong flashlight to create your beam of light.

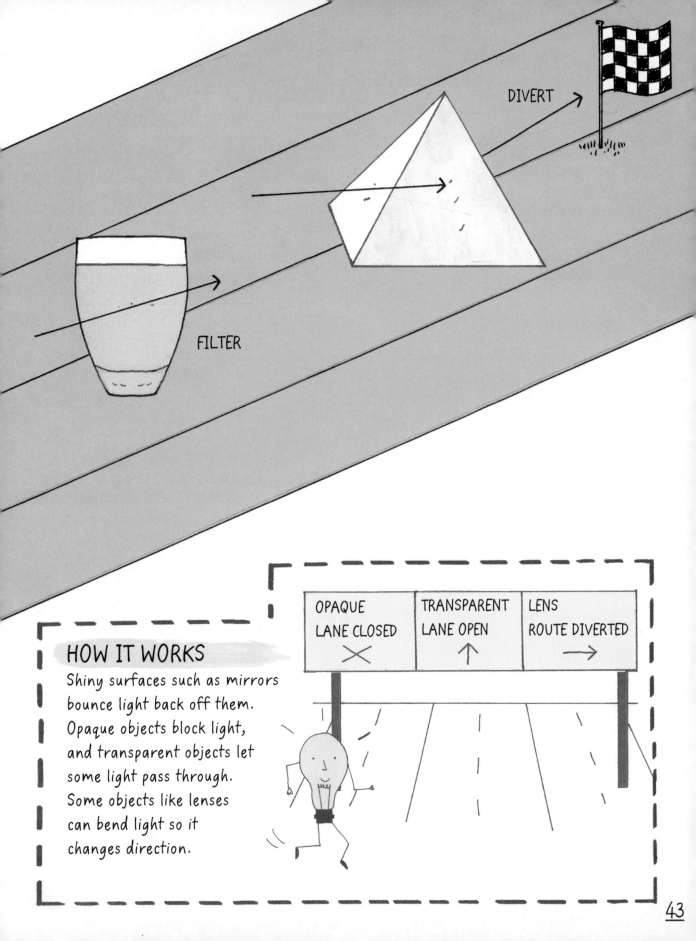

DIVERT

FILTER

HOW IT WORKS

Shiny surfaces such as mirrors bounce light back off them. Opaque objects block light, and transparent objects let some light pass through. Some objects like lenses can bend light so it changes direction.

OPAQUE LANE CLOSED	TRANSPARENT LANE OPEN	LENS ROUTE DIVERTED
✕	↑	→

MAKE WATER FREEZE IN SECONDS

AMAZING!

All you need is a small plastic bottle of fizzy water.

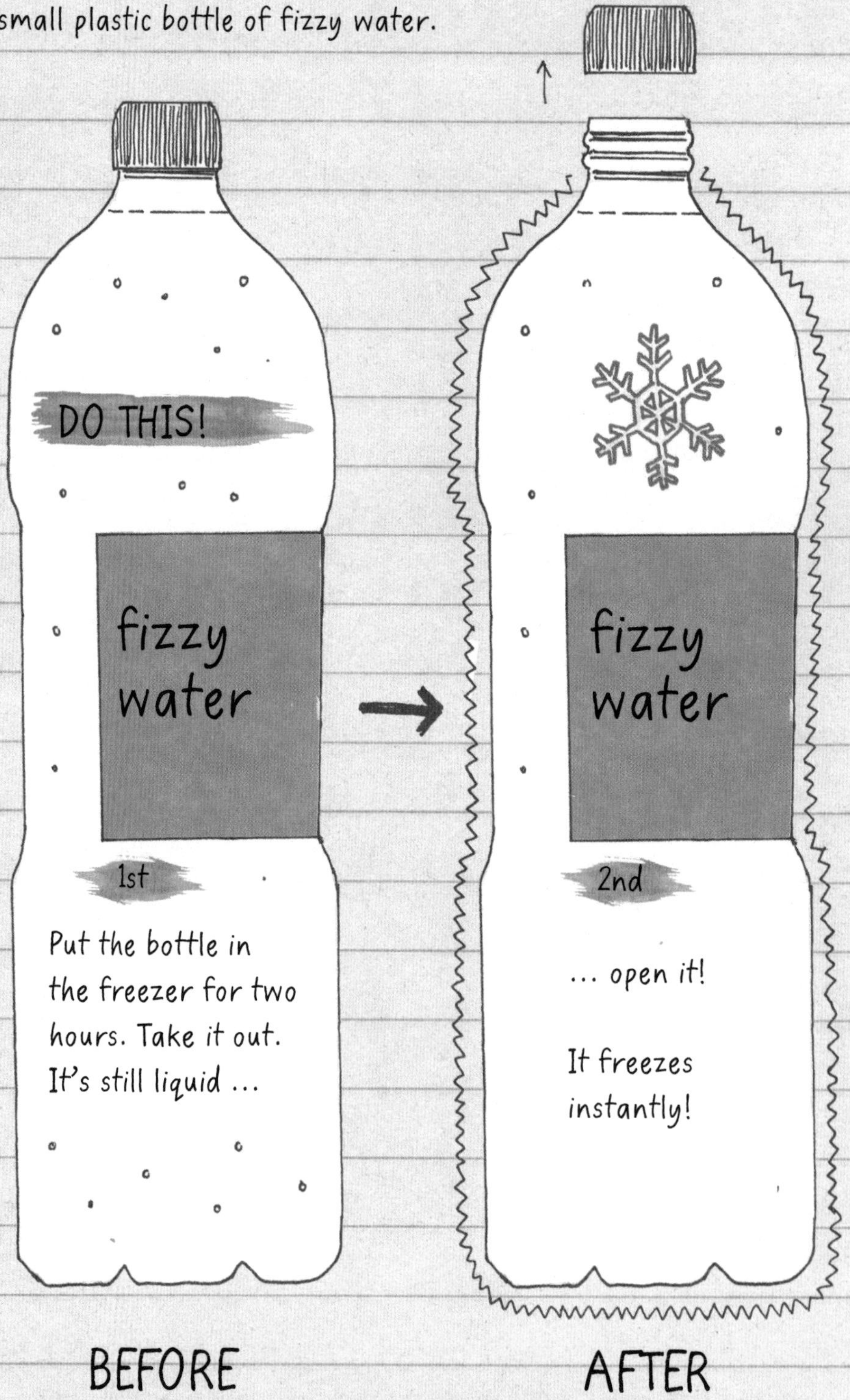

DO THIS!

fizzy water → fizzy water

1st

Put the bottle in the freezer for two hours. Take it out. It's still liquid ...

2nd

... open it!

It freezes instantly!

BEFORE   AFTER

Now experiment with non-fizzy and sugary fizzy drinks. What happens? Does it work?

Watch out for spray!

type of drink	observations	results

HOW IT WORKS

The fizz in fizzy water is carbon dioxide gas. When carbon dioxide is in water, it makes it harder for the water to freeze so the fizzy water stays liquid in the freezer. When the lid comes off, the gas escapes. Water freezes much more easily without gas, and so it turns to ice instantly.

I'm all floaty...

I can't move in here

2 hours

before = liquid with gas

after = solid

CREATE MODERN ART WITH CHROMATOGRAPHY

DO THIS!

1st

Find a coffee filter paper or piece of paper towel,
a selection of water-based colored felt-tips, and
a cup with some water. Cut the paper into strips.

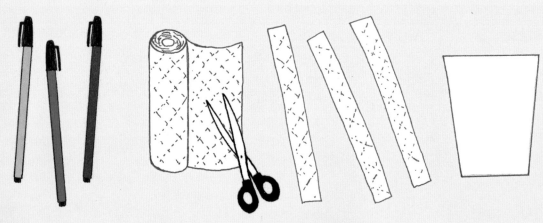

2nd

Color a small solid circle about 1cm
from the end of each paper strip.
(Black is a fun color to test!)

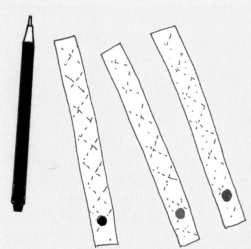

3rd

Pour a little water into a cup, no
more than 0.5cm deep. Put all the
strips in the cup, so the colored
circles are just above the water line
but are NOT touching the water.

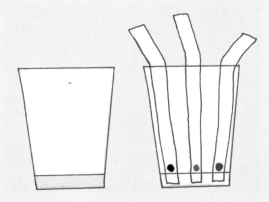

What happens to the ink spots after 10 minutes?

DO THIS!

When the strips have dried, cut out the cool patterns they have created. Stick them here and use them as the start of a piece of modern art.

It's very pretty... but is it art?!

I've no idea, but it's worth MILLIONS!

HOW IT WORKS

Chromatography is a way of separating out mixtures. The ink in your felt-tip is actually made of several different dyes. The water dissolves the ink as it creeps up the paper, and separates out the different colors.

I may look black, but I contain secret colors!

EAT YOUR EXPERIMENT

DO THIS!

1st

Get some chocolate and some ice cream.
Divide each into three portions.

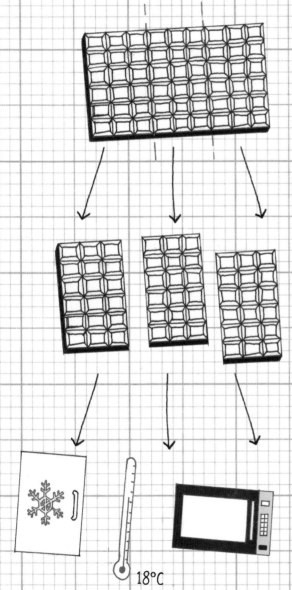

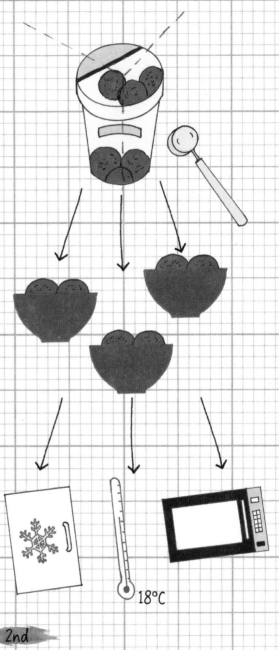

18°C

2nd

Leave one portion of each in the freezer
and one at room temperature for an
hour, and warm one in the microwave
for one minute. Taste each one.

Do they taste different at different temperatures?

18°C

DO THIS!

Describe the taste and texture of the chocolate and the ice cream at each temperature, using as many fancy describing words as possible, like a posh restaurant menu.

This frozen chocolate is quite delectable.

STARTER:
Frozen chocolate with frozen ice cream

MAIN COURSE:
Room temperature chocolate and ice cream

DESSERT:
Warm chocolate and warm ice cream

HOW IT WORKS

The chocolate and the ice cream have different melting points: they turn from a solid to a liquid at different temperatures. But the change from solid to liquid doesn't happen instantly, it is a gradual change. This is why chocolate from the freezer is harder than chocolate at room temperature, even though they are both solid.

At room temperature the ice cream melts, but the chocolate remains solid.

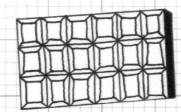

LISTEN TO THE BACKGROUND NOISE

DO THIS!

Shut your eyes for one minute. Listen really carefully. Draw or write down all the sounds you can hear. Are there any you don't normally notice?

PING

I'm whistling while I work!

WHIR

What's the quietest sound you can hear? Try to write the sound as a word.

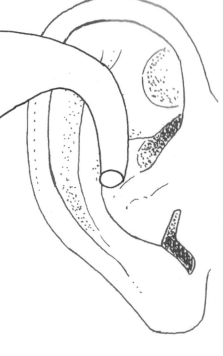

HOW IT WORKS

Sound travels in waves of vibration that jiggle our eardrums and send signals to our brains. But we can't turn our ears off, so after a while our brain filters out background noises, and we stop noticing them.

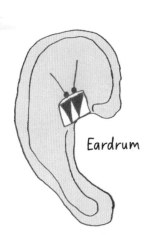

Eardrum

PLAY A DRINKING STRAW LIKE AN OBOE

Wow, I never knew I was musical!

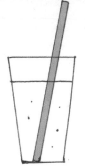

DO THIS!

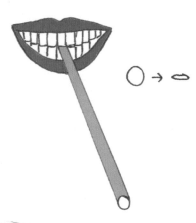

1st
Take a drinking straw and flatten one end by biting down on it and pulling it through your teeth.

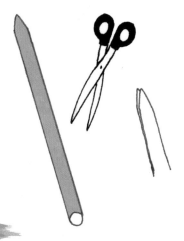

2nd
Snip the corners so the flat end is shaped like a pencil.

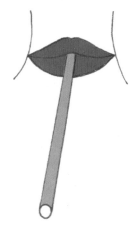

3rd
Put the flat end in your mouth, seal your lips around it, and blow! Try blowing harder and softer until you can make a note.

4th
Try adding finger holes in your straw. Can you make it play different notes?

DO THIS!

Get your friends together and make as many instruments as you can out of bits of rubbish. Can you play a tune you know?

You could name yourselves "The Rubbish Str-orchestra!"

Our music is ext-straw-dinary!

HOW IT WORKS

The cut end of your straw vibrates when you blow. This sends pulses of vibrating air down the straw, which is what makes the noise.

The pitch of the note - how high or low it is - is affected by the frequency of the vibrations (how fast the vibrations are). Faster vibrations make a higher pitched note.

Low pitch

High pitch

DESIGN A NEW MUSICAL INSTRUMENT

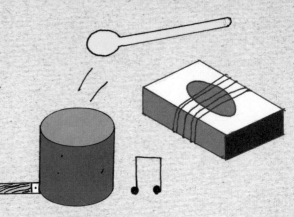

DO THIS!

Invent a musical instrument and draw
it here. Describe the sound it makes.

Make room!

We're twins!

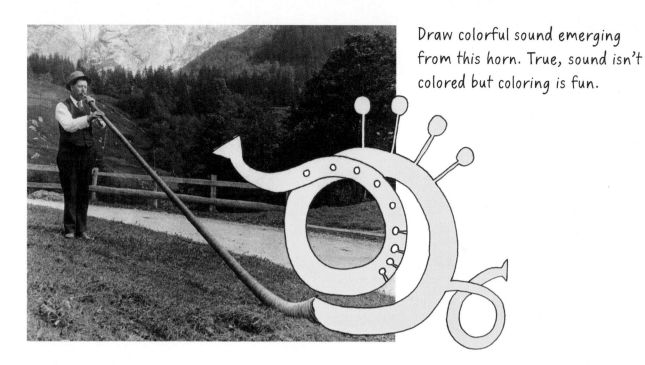

Draw colorful sound emerging from this horn. True, sound isn't colored but coloring is fun.

HOW IT WORKS

Musical instruments make sounds in lots of different ways. Instruments like harps and pianos have strings that vibrate when plucked or hit. Wind instruments such as flutes or trumpets make sound through the vibration of air inside their pipes. Percussion instruments like drums have elastic skins that vibrate when hit.

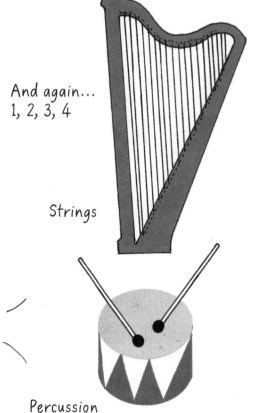

And again...
1, 2, 3, 4

Strings

Percussion

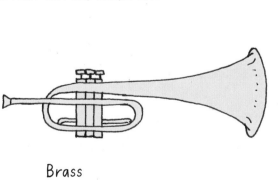

Brass

MAKE SOUNDS WITH THIS BOOK

DO THIS!

Tap, stroke and drum this page
with your fingers or other objects.
What sounds can you make?

Tap here

Brush with your fingers

BANG

Turn to page 89 to make even
more noises using this book!

Drum solo time!

CRASH

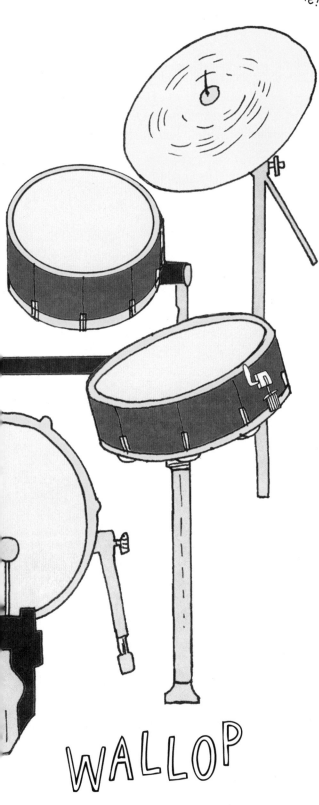

WALLOP

HOW IT WORKS
Drummers use different types of drumsticks to make different noises, from hard wooden sticks, to softer fabric-covered mallets, and wire brushes. These all create different vibrations, affecting the sound of the drum.

I'm a big softie!

INVENT A NEW KIND OF POWER STATION

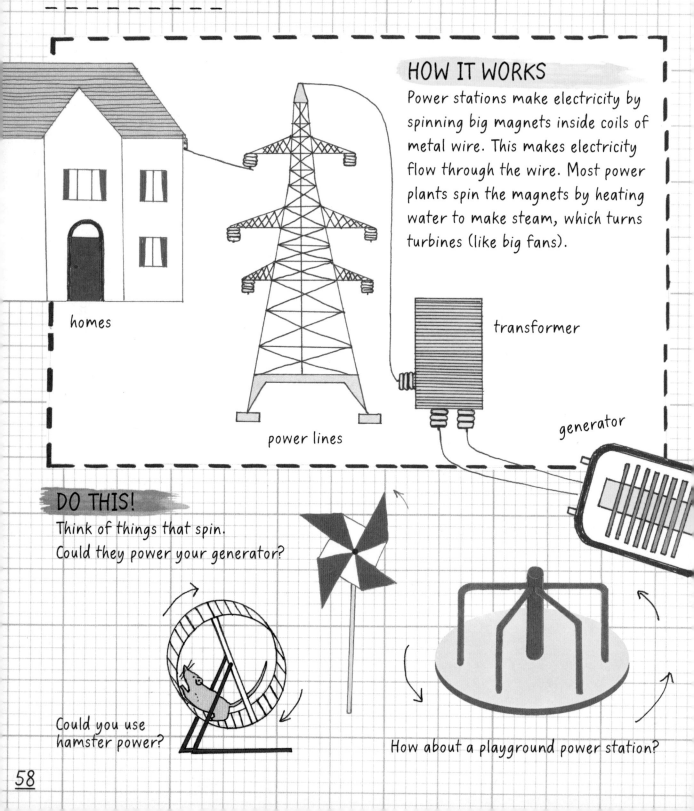

HOW IT WORKS

Power stations make electricity by spinning big magnets inside coils of metal wire. This makes electricity flow through the wire. Most power plants spin the magnets by heating water to make steam, which turns turbines (like big fans).

homes

power lines

transformer

generator

DO THIS!

Think of things that spin.
Could they power your generator?

Could you use hamster power?

How about a playground power station?

Design a way to keep the generator
spinning and producing electricity.

Make this spin!

BEND WATER WITH STATIC POWER

DO THIS!

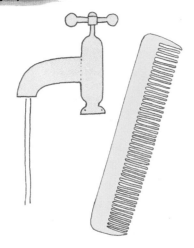

Now that's a powerful style!

1st

Get a plastic comb, and go to the sink. Slowly turn on the tap so you have a very thin stream of water.

2nd

Run the comb through your hair 10 times. Hold the comb close to the water - the flow will start to bend!

HOW IT WORKS

Negatively charged particles called electrons jump from your hair to the comb as you brush it, giving the comb a negative charge. When you put the negatively charged comb near the stream, it is attracted to the positive particles in the water. This pulls the water towards the comb like a magnet.

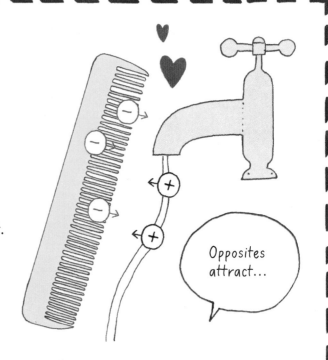

Opposites attract...

DO THIS!

Imagine your static comb is super powerful,
and can attract water on a really big scale.
What could you use it for?

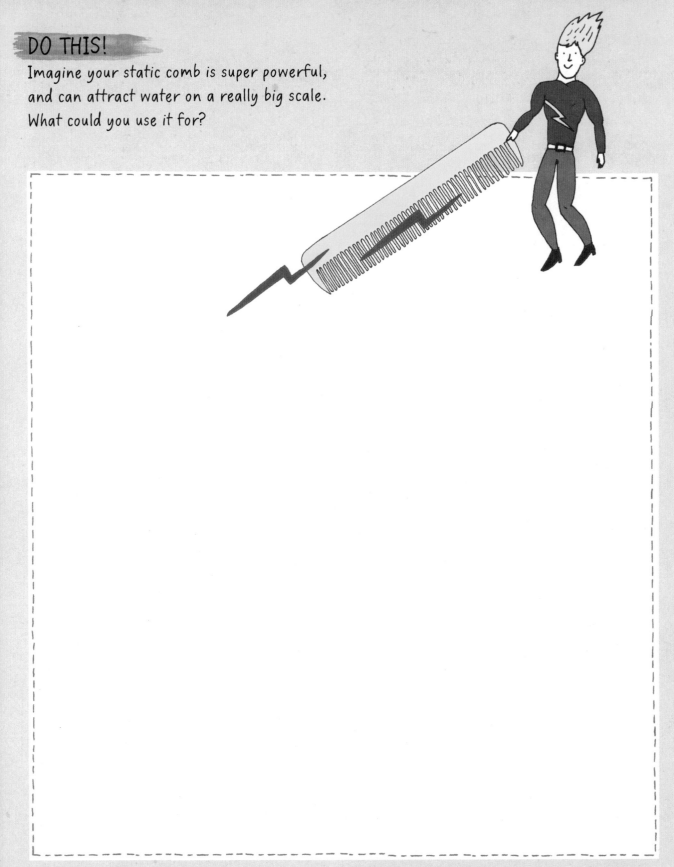

Go to page 95 for more static experiments.

INVESTIGATE ATTRACTION WITH MAGNET TRICKS

DO THIS!

1st

Get a magnet (a fridge magnet would work) a paper clip, and a piece of thread. Tie the paper clip to one end of the thread, and put the other end under something heavy.

What else can you levitate with your magnet?

2nd

Levitate the paper clip by holding the magnet near to it, but just out of reach of the length of the thread.

How far away can you hold the magnet before the paper clip falls?

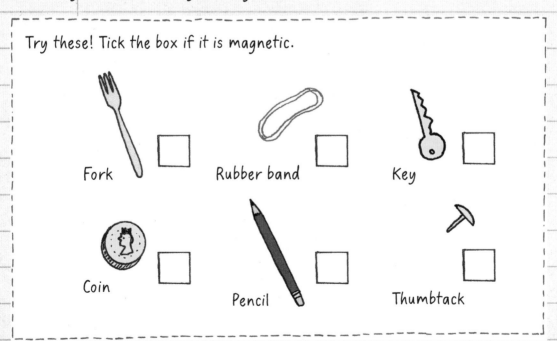

Try these! Tick the box if it is magnetic.

Fork ☐

Rubber band ☐

Key ☐

Coin ☐

Pencil ☐

Thumbtack ☐

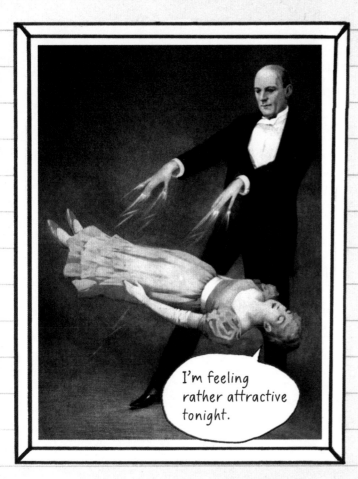

I'm feeling rather attractive tonight.

DO THIS!

Float a flake of cereal (like a cornflake) in a bowl of water. Hold a strong magnet very close above the flake. See if you can make the flake follow the magnet as you move it slowly around the bowl.

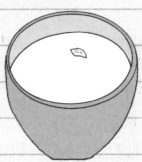

HOW IT WORKS

Magnets create an invisible area around them called a 'magnetic field'. Inside this area, they pull magnetic objects (like your paper clip) towards them. Some cereals contain iron, which is also magnetic. The higher the iron content in your cereal, the better the trick will work.

Is this a magnetic field?

contains iron!

STYLE YOUR HAIR WITH STATIC ELECTRICITY

DO THIS!

1st

Go around your house and rub different objects on your hair. Which materials make your hair stand on end with static electricity?

2nd

Draw your face and hair here, and draw all the objects that make your hair stand on end on the page around them.

You could try:

Hairbrush

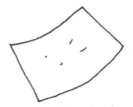

Sheet of paper

MEGA WARNING:
Electricity kills! Never touch electrical sockets.

Draw your face here

Draw your hair here

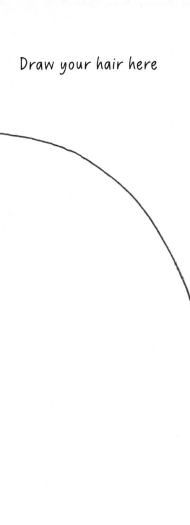

Balloon

Woollen glove

HOW IT WORKS

Some materials shed their electrons
more easily than others, and some
materials pick up extra electrons better.
Dry human hair and skin let go
of their electrons easily.

THIS BOOK THINKS IT'S A LABORATORY

This section is made of portable lab pages for you to cut out and experiment on.

Rip them, snip them, drip on them, and see some science in action!

PAPER PLANE RACE
DO THIS!

Using the next two pages, fold these two models of paper planes and test how well they fly.

The Screech Owl

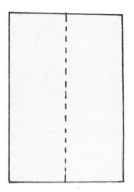

1 Fold paper lengthways

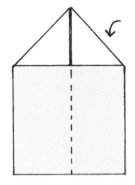

2 Fold top corners in to center

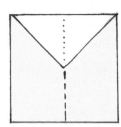

3 Fold top triangle down to make a flat line at the top

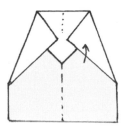

4 Fold top corners in again so the points meet the center line about 6cm from the top

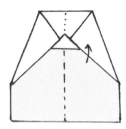

5 Fold the downwards point upwards over the flaps

6 Fold the plane in half and flatten it

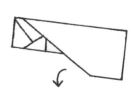

7 Fold the edges down to make wings

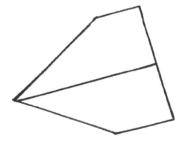

8 This is the shape of the finished plane from above

The Saker Falcon

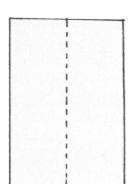

1 Fold paper lengthways

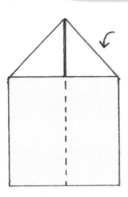

2 Fold top corners in to center

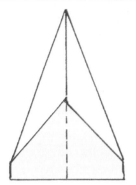

3 Fold sides in to meet the center line again

4 Fold plane in half

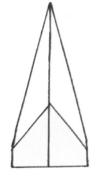

5 Fold the wings down leaving a small body to hold underneath

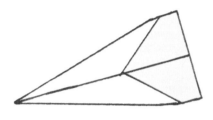

6 The finished plane design

Test both your planes several times.
Record the length of their flights and distance traveled.
Which flies the longest and furthest? Can the designs be improved?

HOW IT WORKS

Several different forces affect the flight of your paper planes in the air. Thrust makes the plane travel forwards. Lift is the force of the air under the planes wings that keeps it up.

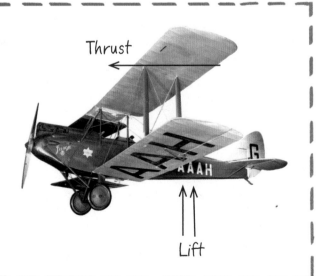

Thrust

Lift

DO THIS!

Cut out these shapes, and test their tessellation on page 23.

DO THIS!

Cut out these tangram pieces, and see if you can recreate the silhouettes on the next page.

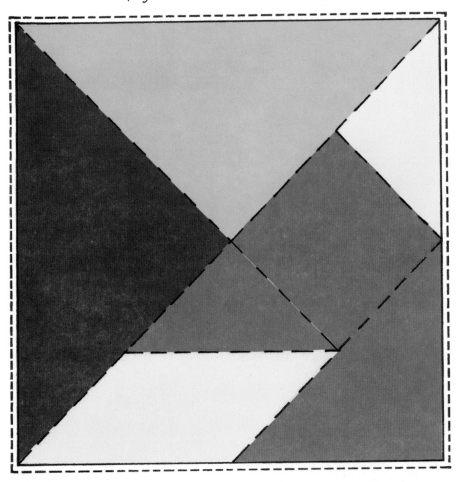

TANGRAM CHALLENGE

DO THIS!

Arrange your tangram pieces so they make these shapes.

Boat

Person

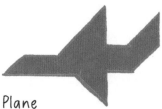

Plane

Swan

Cat

House

Dog

Horse

Rocket

Fish

Rabbit

HOW IT WORKS

The tangram is a geometric puzzle believed to have been invented in China hundreds of years ago. Although it might look simple at first, it's not so easy!

PAPER CRAFT ORRERY

Make a model of the Sun, Earth and Moon.
You'll need two paper fasteners to put it together.

DO THIS!

1st Cut out your orrery pieces on the facing page. Pierce holes in each of the points marked by pushing a sharp pencil through the paper into an eraser.

2nd Use a paper fastener to attach piece 1 (the Earth) on top of piece 2 (the Moon), and attach those on top of piece 3.

3rd Use a second paper fastener to attach the stem of piece 3 to the center of piece 4 (the Sun).

Your orrery goes together like this:

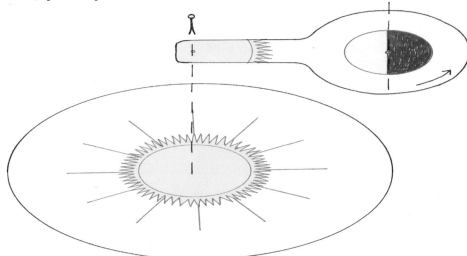

HOW IT WORKS

An orrery is a model of the solar system that shows the movement of the planets around the sun. Your simplified orrery shows the movement of the Moon and Earth around the Sun.

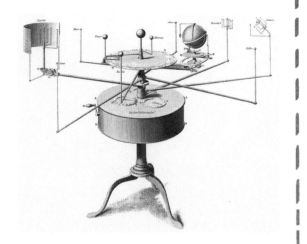

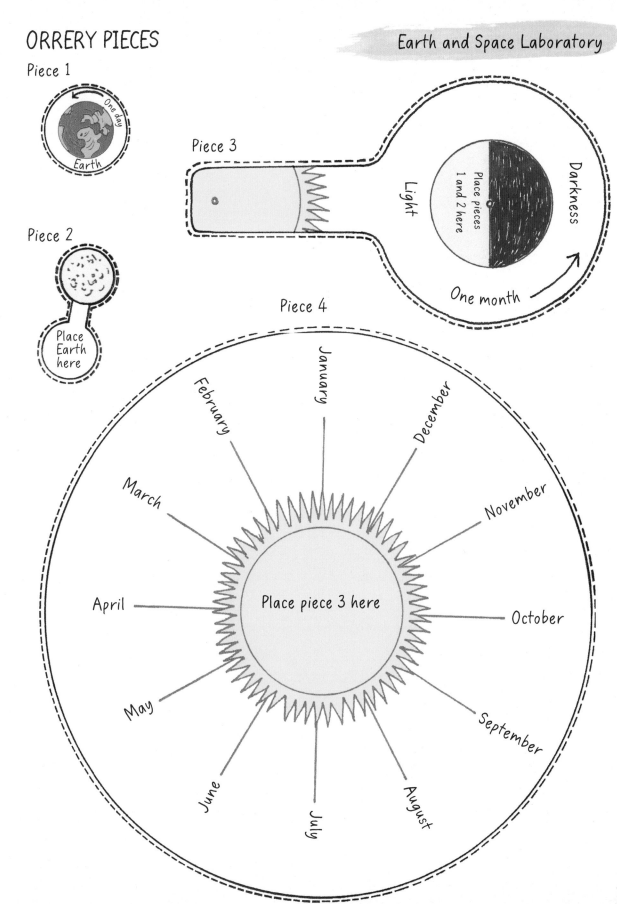

Piece 1

One day

Earth

Piece 3

Light

Place pieces 1 and 2 here

Darkness

One month

Piece 2

Place Earth here

Piece 4

January

February

December

March

November

April

Place piece 3 here

October

May

September

June

July

August

SHADOW PUPPET PLAY

Make shadow puppets to see how light travels.
You'll need a couple of pencils and tape, and a flashlight or desk lamp.

DO THIS!

1st

Cut out these shapes, and fix handles
to them by taping a pencil on the back.

2nd

In a dark room, hold them in front
of the flashlight or lamp beam,
to cast shadows on the wall.
Move the puppets closer to and
further away from the light.
Try holding the puppets at an
angle. What do you notice?
What happens if you add a
light source in another place?

HOW IT WORKS

Light travels in straight lines, and opaque things block it from passing. But why do shadows have fuzzy edges? This is because light sources like your flashlight are sending out light rays from all over their surface. The fuzzy edges of the shadow are where some light rays have been blocked, but others haven't.

DROP RACE DRIP TEST

DO THIS!

Cut this page out and lie it flat. Drop blobs of the liquids on each star.

Hold the page up so the liquids drip. Try to predict the winner before you start!

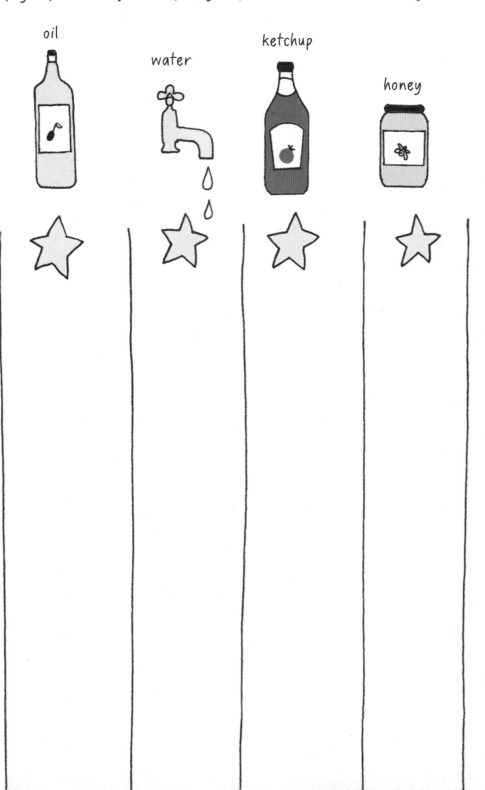

oil

water

ketchup

honey

DROPS MAZE

DO THIS!

Choose the liquid you think will be easiest
to steer and guide a drop around the maze.

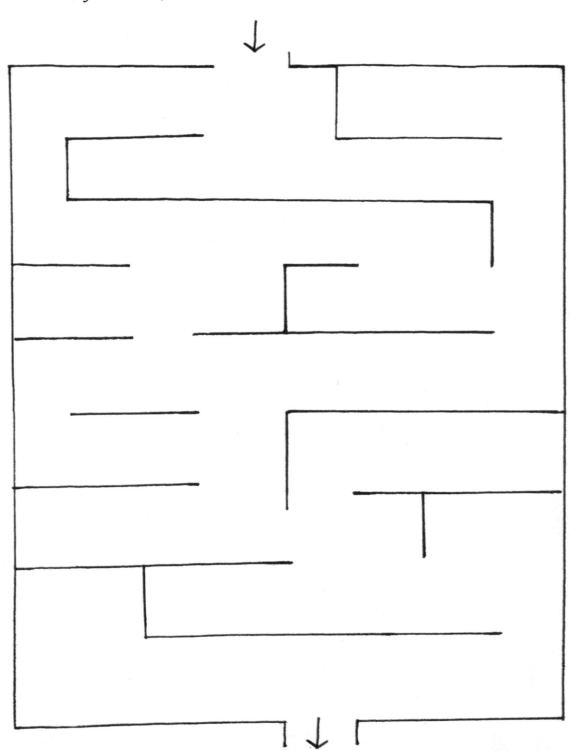

DRIP TESTS: THE RESULTS

Which drop was the fastest?
Write the results here:

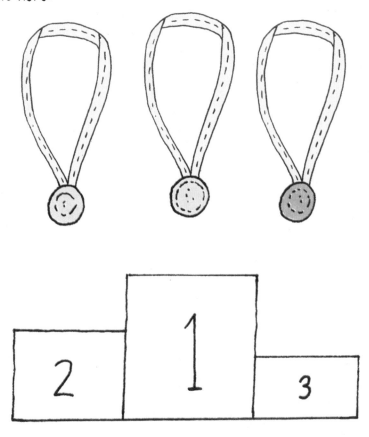

HOW IT WORKS

Honey is thicker, or more viscous, than water. When you measure how fast a liquid flows, you measure its viscosity.

Viscosity depends partly on how easy it is for the molecules in the liquid to slide over each other. Molecules containing only a few atoms slide over each other more easily than molecules with lots of atoms.

SOAP SPEED BOAT

Use this cool surface-tension trick to make a paper boat whizz along!
You'll need a large tub or bath of water and some liquid soap.

DO THIS!

1st Cut out the boat shape opposite. Place it gently at one end of a large tub of water so it floats.

2nd Very carefully drip some liquid soap right behind the motor piece sticking out at the back.

The boat should whizz forwards along the water.

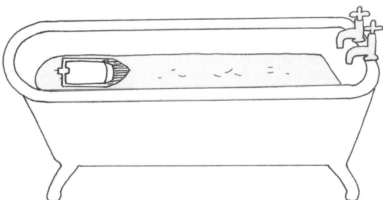

HOW IT WORKS

Molecules at the water's surface stick together extra strongly. This makes a sort of "skin" called "surface tension." Soap breaks down the surface tension, and as it breaks the skin it creates enough of a force to push the boat forwards.

There's a lot of tension between us

Hmm... have you tried soap?

Cut out, then gently crease but don't flatten along the center line.

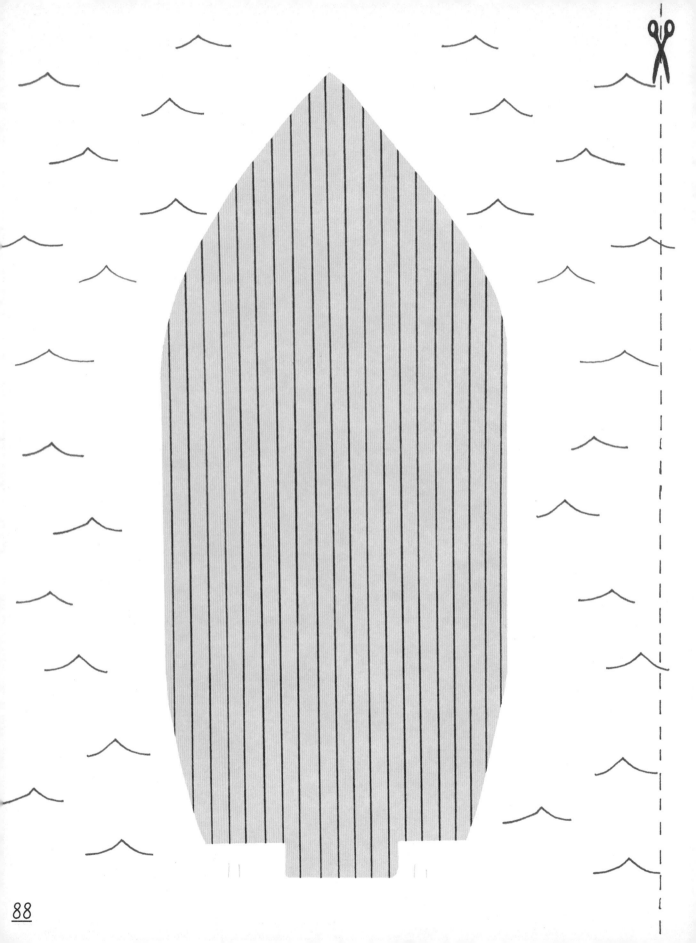

SOUND TEST PART 2

DO THIS!

Use this page to make as many different
noises as you can. Rip it, crumple it,
yank it, go crazy...

tear here

crumple here

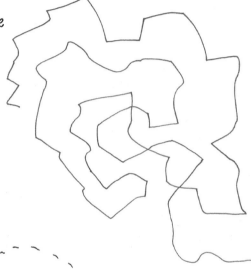

riffle!

rumple!

yank here

1, 2, 1, 2, testing, testing...

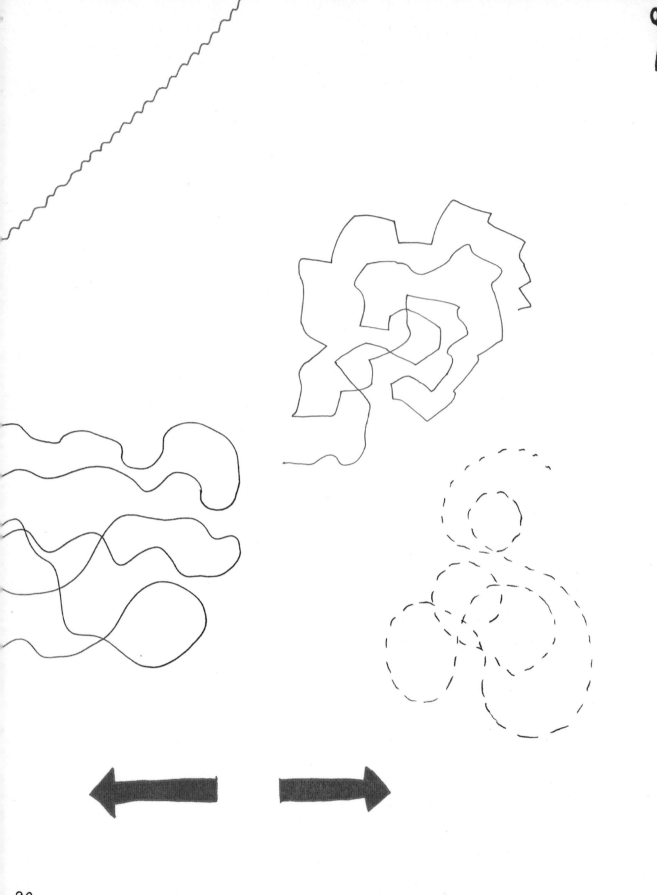

PAPER SOUND MACHINES

DO THIS!

Make yourself really (un)popular with these noisy paper squeaker and popper crafts.

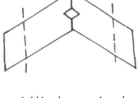

2 Snip a little triangle shape out of the middle of the folded edge

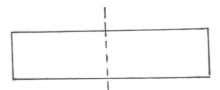

1 Find a strip of paper about 3 inches by 8 inches, and fold it in half lengthways

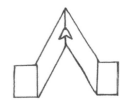

3 Fold the ends out to make finger holders

4 Place a finger on each end of the squeaker, hold it against closed lips, and blow through until you make the most annoying noise possible. Silly faces optional.

HOW IT WORKS

As air moves through it, the pressure inside the squeaker drops. Higher pressure outside the squeaker pushes the sides inwards, shutting off the air. With the air shut off, the sides pop outwards again. This happens over and over again very fast, and this vibration makes the squeaking noise.

Hey, it isn't me!

DO THIS!

Use the next page to make an origami paper popper.

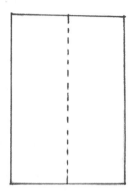

1 Fold paper lengthways

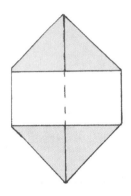

2 Fold all four corners to the center line

3 Fold in half down the center line and flatten

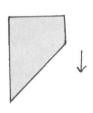

4 Fold the top point down to meet the bottom point

5 Fold the top point back on itself to make a triangle

6 Turn it over and fold the other point up to make a smaller triangle

Front

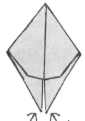

two points

7 Your popper should look like this from the front

Side

Open up top flap a little bit here

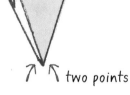

two points

8 Hold it by the two points, and pull the inside piece out a little bit to make it easier to pop

SNAP!

9 Flick your wrist downwards quickly so the fold pops open and makes a snapping noise

STICKY PAPER TRICK

DO THIS!

1st Tear this page up into teeny-weeny little pieces. As small as you possibly can. Yes, this very page! Put the pieces on a flat surface.

Rip me up into teeny tiny pieces!

2nd Find a plastic comb or balloon, and rub it with wool or on your hair to charge it with static electricity. Hold it closely over the paper pieces and watch them dance!

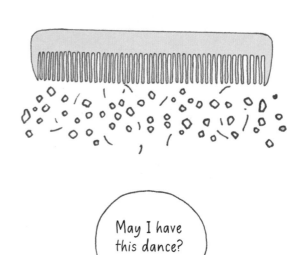

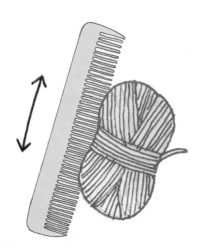

May I have this dance?

Goodbye!